LONDON'S NEW
ROUTEMASTERS

LONDON'S NEW ROUTEMASTERS

DAVID BEDDALL

AMBERLEY

Acknowledgements

I would like to thank Liam Farrer-Beddall, Gary Seamarks and Luke Garley for allowing me to use images from their photograph collections. I would also like to thank my wife, Helen, for her continuing support and patience during the production of this book. Lastly, I would like to thank my parents, Mary and William, for also supporting me while producing this book.

First published 2019

Amberley Publishing
The Hill, Stroud
Gloucestershire, GL5 4EP

www.amberley books.com

Copyright © David Beddall, 2019

The right of David Beddall to be identified as the Authors of this work has been asserted in accordance with the Copyright, Designs and Patents Act 1988.

ISBN 978 1 4456 8738 4 (print)
ISBN 978 1 4456 8739 1 (ebook)

British Library Cataloguing in Publication Data. A catalogue record for this book is available from the British Library.

Origination by Amberley Publishing.
Printed in the UK.

Introduction

In his electoral pledge, Boris Johnson said that he wanted to dispose of the bendibus and introduce a new, modern version of the Routemaster. When elected, he fulfilled this promise by launching a competition to both the public and the design industry to create the new vehicle. On 18 December 2009, Wrightbus of Ballymena was announced as the successful bidder, using the design produced by Heatherwick Studios. A full mock-up was unveiled to the public at London Transport Museum's Acton Town depot in November 2010.

It took a further year before the first production model, LT1, was officially launched at Trafalgar Square on 16 December 2011. The vehicle became known officially as the New Bus for London (NBfL) and gained the unofficial name of the 'Borismaster'. LT1 went on for further testing at various locations, including the Milbrook proving ground in Bedfordshire. This became the first new bus that was specifically designed for operation in the capital.

Route 38 between Victoria and Clapton Pond was the route chosen to trial eight prototype New Buses for London machines. LT2 became the first example to enter service on 27 February 2012, operating from Ash Grove garage rather than Clapton garage, where the rest of the 38 was operated from. Arriva London took control of the vehicles with a small, dedicated team of staff.

Boris Johnson was re-elected in 2012 and an order for 600 NBfL machines was placed. The first of these vehicles arrived in the capital in June 2013 and entered service on route 24 between Pimlico and Hampstead Heath. It was decided that the NBfL machines should be registered in a special Northern Ireland registration sequence with the prefix LTZ. A handful of the 24 batch were delivered with London registration plates.

The first three prototypes, LT1–3, embarked on a world tour in May 2013. Lasting just over a year, LT2 and LT3 returned to the United Kingdom in August 2014, with LT1 returning later in the year. Upon arrival back in the country, LT2 went on loan to First West Yorkshire for a six-month trial. It was painted green and branded as the New Bus for West Yorkshire. However, it was not used in service there; instead, it was only displayed at various events in the area. It returned to London in 2015. Further examples, LT312/3, were placed on loan during November 2014, this time in the Dundee area, operating with Stagecoach Strathtay.

A further 200 examples were ordered in 2014, bringing the total up to 808 examples, although this was slightly reduced to 805. January 2016 saw 195 more examples ordered, taking the total of NBfL/New Routemasters (NRM) in London service to a round 1,000. The final examples were taken into stock by the end of 2017.

Although production of the New Bus for London ceased after the 1,000th example was taken into stock, a similar version was constructed, which was named the Wright

SRM. Described as a vehicle that was designed for use around the whole country rather than just London, the SRM was similar in appearance to the NBfL but with the absence of the rear staircase. Based on the Volvo B5LH chassis, the first six examples were taken into stock by London Sovereign in September 2016, who put them to use on route 13 between Golders Green and Aldwych. Two further examples were completed to Transport for London (TfL) specification on the B5LHC chassis, which are due to be trialled in London in the near future. They were delivered to Go-Ahead London for use from London Central's Peckham garage. These vehicles are charged using a pantograph rather than the traditional method, giving them a trolleybus-like appearance.

The first prototype, LT1 (LT61 AHT), was one of eight examples put to use from Ash Grove garage to operate the 38. It is seen passing through a wet Cambridge Circus, bound for Victoria. The vehicle was later re-registered LTZ 1001. (Liam Farrer-Beddall)

After a six-month loan to First West Yorkshire, LT2 was painted into a green livery. When it returned to London, it was decided to keep the vehicle in this green livery and apply London Transport fleet names along with gold Arriva names. It is seen heading towards Victoria in Hackney Central. (Liam Farrer-Beddall)

A different view of Hyde Park Corner from many that will appear in this book, showing Knightsbridge taking traffic down to Kensington, and to the right of the photograph an arch leading into Hyde Park itself. The London Underground sign is also visible in this photograph. LT3 is seen carrying its original registration (LT61 CHT) while bound for Clapton Pond on route 38. (Gary Seamarks)

The forecourt of Clapton garage finds LT4 sporting registration LTZ 1004. It was delivered to Arriva in May 2012 and originally carried registration LT12 DHT. A number of the New Bus for London machines have been adorned with all-over advertisements since their introduction to London, with LT4 carrying more than most. A scheme in the autumn of 2016 saw the vehicle gain one to promote tourism to Switzerland. (Liam Farrer-Beddall)

The last of the prototypes arrived in July 2012. Originally registered LT12 HHT, it was placed into service with Arriva London on the 38. In June 2014, the vehicle found its way to Holloway garage under the care of Metroline. Bound for Lancaster Gate on service 390, LTZ 1008 is seen travelling down Oxford Street. (Liam Farrer-Beddall)

Three of the original production batch of NBfL vehicles were registered in the LK13 series, being registered early for type familiarisation duties. LT11 (LK 13FJJ) was one such vehicle and is seen rounding Trafalgar Square shortly after the conversion of route 24 to the type on a sunny day in June 2013. (Liam Farrer-Beddall)

Notting Hill Gate used to be served by two LT services, the 148 and 390. The latter route was rerouted to replace the 73 between Oxford Circus and Victoria. Metroline's LT12 (LTZ 1012) is seen on layover at Notting Hill Gate wearing a multicoloured all-over advertisement for Red Bull's Culture Clash. LT12 formed part of the first production batch ordered against the contract on route 24, but with both services being allocated to Holloway garage, interworking on the 24 and 390 is commonplace. (Liam Farrer-Beddall)

Hampstead Heath finds LT19 (LTZ 1019) on a sunny June day in 2013. LT19 was one of the first thirty-two production models of the NBfL introduced to route 24 (Pimlico–Hampstead Heath) in June 2013. The destination on this vehicle suggests that it performed a short working to Chalk Farm. (Liam Farrer-Beddall)

Route 24 takes in a number of tourist sites in the City of Westminster. One such location is Parliament Square, where we find LT27 (LTZ 1027) heading towards Hampstead Heath. Another New Routemaster can be seen in the background advertising YouTube. (Gary Seamarks)

The front seats of an NBfL provide a good vantage point for taking photographs. Such a technique was used to capture LT34 (LTZ 1034), which is seen passing Mornington Crescent Underground station. It is seen heading towards Pimlico while advertising the *Charlie and the Chocolate Factory* show. (Liam Farrer-Beddall)

The early batches of NBfL vehicles delivered to London operators featured a colourful logo as opposed to the generic white logo of later batches. The yellow Go-Ahead London fleet name is clearly displayed on LT45, which is seen passing through Victoria en route to Fulham Broadway on route 11. This vehicle was part of a twenty-eight-strong batch taken into stock for the conversion of route 11 to the type in September 2013. This batch found themselves allocated to London General's Stockwell garage. (Liam Farrer-Beddall)

LT50 (LTZ 1050) is seen approaching the stop near Victoria bus station. It is seen heading towards Liverpool Street station from Fulham Broadway while decorated in a more basic all-over advertisement for Sky Q, which it gained in February 2016. (Liam Farrer-Beddall)

This photograph shows a general view of the area around the bus stop named 'St Paul's Churchyard'. It is at this location we find LT53 (LTZ 1053) loading passengers before completing a shorter journey on route 11 to Chelsea, World's End. (Gary Seamarks)

The infamous IMAX Cinema at Waterloo can be seen in the background of this photograph of LT59 (LTZ 1059). This vehicle is seen travelling out of service, displaying 'Transport for London' on its destination displays, along with the roundel on the front destination display. The three-doored layout of the type can be clearly seen in this view. (Liam Farrer-Beddall)

LT60 (LTZ 1060) was decorated into the pre-war-style General livery in October 2014 and has retained this livery. Passing through Aldwych, it is seen operating a shorting working of route 11, terminating at Chelsea, World's End, instead of Fulham Broadway. (Liam Farrer-Beddall)

LT62 (LTZ 1062) is most notable for being involved in a serious accident on Chelsea Bridge in September 2013. The damage was so severe that it was sent back to Wrightbus for rebuild, returning to Go-Ahead London in March 2016. Due to its absence, another LT was allocated to London General to replace LT62. Upon its return to London, it was reallocated to Camberwell garage, where it was used on route 12. It is seen operating this service towards the Dulwich Library terminus, passing through Elephant and Castle. (Liam Farrer-Beddall)

A number of London bus services use York Road at the side of King's Cross station as a stand. One such route is the 10, as demonstrated by LT74 (LTZ 1074). Other services also use this road to access North London. (Gary Seamarks)

Seen on its intended route is LT79 (LTZ 1079). Having set off from its Aldwych terminus, this vehicle is seen passing through Trafalgar Square towards Hammersmith. The position of the centre staircase can be clearly seen in this photograph, with the second being hidden behind the panels at the rear of the vehicle. (Liam Farrer-Beddall)

A wet Hammersmith finds LT90 (LTZ 1090). The small spotlights fitted to the interior can be glimpsed through the top-deck window, and the unique headlight style can also be clearly seen. (Liam Farrer-Beddall)

Route 24 passes through some of the capitals many tourist attractions, including Parliament Square, Whitehall, Trafalgar Square and Camden Town. The latter area finds LT96 (LTZ 1096), one of twenty-three machines taken into stock to convert route 390 to the type. Metroline's Holloway garage took stock of these vehicles, and LT96 clearly shows the common user pool approach adopted by Metroline. (Liam Farrer-Beddall)

Between October and December 2016, Metroline's LT97 (LTZ 1097) carried an all-over advertising livery for West End show *Half a Sixpence*. This smart blue-based livery is captured when LT97 pauses briefly on Oxford Street. (Liam Farrer-Beddall)

Above and below: Metroline's LT100 (LTZ 1100) has for most of its career carried an advertisement for guitar maker Fender. The advert was slightly amended on a couple of occasions and we see two variations of this campaign on the vehicle. Above, it is seen having just loaded at Oxford Street while operating on route 390, doing a short working to Lancaster Gate. Below, it is seen round Trafalgar Square while operating route 24 to Hampstead Heath. (Liam Farrer-Beddall)

Another example of the route 390 batch seen on route 24. LT98 (LTZ 1098) is seen in a pink advertising wrap for Propper Popcorn while travelling through Victoria towards Hampstead Heath. (Liam Farrer-Beddall)

LT102 (LTZ 1102) is seen having just passed St Pancras International en route for Archway. The St Pancras/King's Cross area is a prime spot for services operated by the NBfL, with five routes (10, 59, 73, 91 and 390) passing through the area. The various locations around the area provide some interesting backdrops to photographs, some of which will be seen later in this book. (Liam Farrer-Beddall)

As mentioned earlier, route 390 was rerouted on 17 June 2017 from Notting Hill Gate to Victoria, diverting at Marble Arch, then running down Park Lane instead of Bayswater Road, through Hyde Park Corner to Victoria. The new destination is shown off by LT104 (LTZ 1104), which is seen near journey's end at Victoria. (Liam Farrer-Beddall)

The parking area at the rear of Archway station provides a layover point for a number of services terminating at Archway itself. This location finds LT106 (LTZ 1106) displaying the not in service blind used by the NBfL machines. (Liam Farrer-Beddall)

Wall's Ice Cream placed several designs on the New Bus for London machines in subsequent years. To promote the new black and pink Magnum lollies, several examples gained a black and pink livery. One such example was LT111 (LTZ 1111), which is seen passing through Victoria on route 24. (Liam Farrer-Beddall)

Marble Arch is another area served by a number of NBfL routes. LT113 (LTZ 1113) is seen passing through this location, heading towards Notting Hill Gate on route 390. A comparison with the traditional Routemaster can be made in this photograph. (Liam Farrer-Beddall)

LT118 (LTZ 1118) was bought in to replace accident-damaged LT62 on route 11 at Stockwell. It is seen operating a short service to Chelsea, World's End, passing the Royal Courts of Justice on Fleet Street, just before it passes through the Aldwych. (Gary Seamarks)

Route 148 (Shepherds Bush–Camberwell Green) was the fifth route to be converted to the type in February 2014. The twenty-five vehicles required to operate the service were allocated to London United's Shepherds Bush garage. LT120 (LTZ 1120) is seen rounding Hyde Park Corner as it heads towards Shepherds Bush while sporting an advertising wrap for the Samsung S8 mobile phone. (Liam Farrer-Beddall)

Having just crossed Westminster Bridge, LT123 (LTZ 1123) is seen heading towards Camberwell Green. Big Ben features prominently in the background of this photograph. A Wright Eclipse Gemini 2 machine can be glimpsed in the background on route 12, a service that will be converted to the New Routemaster the following year. (Liam Farrer-Beddall)

As seen in the previous photograph, route 148 passes a number of famous London landmarks. LT126 (LTZ 1126) is seen about to pass through Marble Arch, having just exited Bayswater Road as it heads towards Camberwell Green. (Liam Farrer-Beddall)

Another shot taken at Hyde Park Corner, again of another New Routemaster in an all-over advertisement wrap. LT136 (LTZ 1136) is seen promoting Campo Viejo wine while basking in the sunshine. (Liam Farrer-Beddall)

The year 2014 was declared the 'Year of the Bus' by Transport for London. Numerous events were organised across the capital to commemorate this. Ten New Routemaster vehicles had a special silver livery along with Year of the Bus logos applied to them. The first vehicle to be treated to this livery was LT150 (LTZ 1150), which was added to London United's fleet. It is seen near journey's end passing through Trafalgar Square on route 9. (Liam Farrer-Beddall)

Route 10 gained an allocation of New Routemasters in April 2014. Placed into service with London United from Stamford Brook garage, the allocation was soon intermixed with those operating on route 9, as is demonstrated here. Both routes 9 and 10 terminate at Hammersmith bus station, where LT156 (LTZ 1156) is seen on layover on a winter's evening. The distinctive headlights of these vehicles are shown off in this photograph. (Liam Farrer-Beddall)

LT159 (LTZ 1159) is seen on the correct route, the 10 (Hammersmith–King's Cross). The New Routemaster has appeared in many different colours for advertisements, but pink was not as commonly used. It is seen crossing Euston Road just before serving Euston train station. (Liam Farrer-Beddall)

A wet Hammersmith bus station finds LT166 (LTZ 1166) having just offloaded its passengers after completing a journey from King's Cross. It was originally intended that the rear door of these vehicles would open fully to give the effect of an open platform. This was soon altered as seen in this photograph, where the smaller section of the door remains closed. (Liam Farrer-Beddall)

It took a while for route 38 to gain a full allocation of the New Routemaster vehicles. No less than sixty-three examples were taken into stock to operate the service, topped up by seven of the eight prototypes. LT186 is seen passing the back end of Buckingham Palace, heading towards Victoria bus station. It is displaying the second advertising campaign for Coca-Cola – one that was applied to numerous vehicles of the type. (Liam Farrer-Beddall)

During the summer of 2014, two experimental New Routemasters split up the batch delivered for route 38, with one each going to London General and Metroline. The latter operator gained LT190 (LTZ 1190), which is seen rounding Hyde Park Corner while wearing the special silver livery. Allocated to Cricklewood garage, this vehicle was predominantly used on route 16 between the garage and Victoria. This was one of the last vehicles to carry the silver livery, retaining it long after the others had been repainted. (Liam Farrer-Beddall)

Over the summer of 2014, adidas launched a big advertising campaign on the New Routemaster vehicles to promote their involvement in the World Cup. After this, a handful of NRMs had their livery changed to promote the adidas store in London. One such vehicle was LT192 (LTZ 1192), which was redecorated blue with white stripes, making use of the front staircase. It is seen heading toward Victoria, passing through Holborn. (Liam Farrer-Beddall)

Upon conversion, route 38 was allocated to Clapton garage, located near to Hackney Central. Passing near to the entrance of its home garage is LT195 (LTZ 1195). Many of the New Routemasters carried side adverts for West End shows, with this example carrying one for the *Book of Mormon*. (Liam Farrer-Beddall)

LT215 (LTZ 1215) is seen exiting Clapton garage. The black adidas livery was applied to thirty-five New Routemasters and is seen clearly in this view. The campaign featured various football stars on the sides of the vehicles, each one being different. Arriva London operated the majority of the black New Routemasters. (Liam Farrer-Beddall)

Another shot taken in Hackney Central. This time, LT222 (LTZ 1222) is found travelling down Amhurst Road, Hackney. This is now the route all buses take as a result of the pedestrianisation of Mare Street. Route 48, as seen in the background, was another route to be converted to New Routemaster. (Liam Farrer-Beddall)

Another different view of Hyde Park Corner, this time looking towards the Victoria area. Here we find LT230 (LTZ 1230) operating route 38 towards Clapton Pond. This route passes down Piccadilly to Piccadilly Circus, then through Cambridge Circus and Centre Point before heading out to Clapton Pond. (Gary Seamarks)

A reduction in the PVR of several routes allowed the cascade of several New Routemasters to begin the conversion of routes 48 (Walthamstow–London Bridge) and 254 (Aldgate–Holloway). In time, route 137 also received a newer batch of New Routemasters, with the existing vehicles from that route moving across to these two services too. Former route 38 LT234 (LTZ 1234) is seen operating route 254 and was allocated to Ash Grove garage. It is seen passing Finsbury Park station en route to Aldgate. (Liam Farrer-Beddall)

One of the more iconic liveries worn by a New Routemaster was the 'Ride with Pride' livery applied to LT239 (LTZ 1239) in March 2015 in support of the LGBT trust. It attended many events while sporting this livery and is seen here attending Bromley garage open day. (Liam Farrer-Beddall)

Another view of St Paul's Churchyard stop. This time we find Stagecoach London's LT240 (LTZ 1240) pausing to load a sizable crowd while operating a journey on the 15 towards Trafalgar Square. (Gary Seamarks)

Several routes operated by New Routemasters pass through Bishopsgate, close to Liverpool Street station, including the 8. This is where we find LT251 (LTZ 1251) on a sunny summer's afternoon soon after the route was converted to the type. (Liam Farrer-Beddall)

Seen travelling in the opposite direction down Bishopsgate is Stagecoach London's LT253 (LTZ 1253). This was another example of the black adidas advertising wrap, and as mentioned previously, a different player is featured on the side of this vehicle compared with the route 38 example. (Liam Farrer-Beddall)

The initial all-over advertisements were applied to the New Routemasters at Bus & Coach World in Blackburn, Lancashire. This is where we find Stagecoach London's LT254 (LTZ 1254) being prepared for the adidas campaign. (David Beddall)

Holborn is another good location to capture New Routemasters, with routes 8, 38, 55, 59, 68, 91 and 168 passing through. It is at this location where LT258 (LTZ 1258) is captured nearing journey's end at Tottenham Court Road station. (Liam Farrer-Beddall)

Oxford Street is another busy location for the New Routemaster type, with many routes either travelling down it or crossing it at Oxford Circus. Seen a short distance from Tottenham Court Road station is LT261 (LTZ 1261). (Liam Farrer-Beddall)

Several New Routemaster services pass the doors of St Paul's Cathedral (11, 15 and 76). All travel down the hill past City Thameslink station and on to Ludgate Circus and Fleet Street. Seen heading in that direction is LT267 (LTZ 1267), which is operating route 15 to Trafalgar Square. The distinctive dome of St Paul's can be clearly seen. (Gary Seamarks)

It has become a tradition that Transport for London would allow a handful of London buses each year to be decorated in a poppy livery to commemorate Armistice Day in November. The chosen vehicle in 2014 was LT269 (LTZ 1269), which is seen parked in the Aldwych having just taken part in the Lord Mayor's Show parade. (Liam Farrer-Beddall)

October 2014 saw the conversion of Go-Ahead London's route 453 from Enviro 400 machines to the New Routemaster. The route runs between Deptford Bridge DLR station and Marylebone station and requires thirty-five vehicles at peak times. LT274 (LTZ 1274) is seen approaching Trafalgar Square. The initial allocation of these vehicles was to Mandela Way garage, but when this garage closed in 2017 the batch was moved to nearby New Cross. (Liam Farrer-Beddall)

The 453 is one of a handful of routes to cross Oxford Street at the junction with Oxford Circus. This is where we find LT287 (LTZ 1287), which is heading towards Deptford Bridge. (Liam Farrer-Beddall)

Elephant and Castle finds LT298 (LTZ 1298) heading towards Marylebone. This vehicle briefly carried an advertising wrap for GiGi in early 2017, which it is seen wearing in this photograph. (Liam Farrer-Beddall)

Route 453 passes by the entrance to New Cross bus garage. It is at this location where we find LT301 (LTZ 1301) pulling off the stop just after loading passengers for its trip into Central London. (Liam Farrer-Beddall)

Seen travelling through Waterloo not in service, despite the blinds reading rail replacement, is Go-Ahead London's LT306 (LTZ 1306). It is seen wearing a bright yellow all-over advertisement for Chiquta Bananas. (Liam Farrer-Beddall)

LT312 (LTZ 1312) was one of a pair of New Routemasters delivered directly to Stagecoach Strathtay at Dundee for trials around the area in November 2014. The pair arrived in London in December and were allocated to Stagecoach London's Leyton garage for use on route 55 between Bakers Arms, Leyton, and Oxford Circus. Wearing an advertisement for Coca-Cola, it is captured about to enter Oxford Street. (Liam Farrer-Beddall)

Five LTs were taken into stock out of sequence by Stagecoach London in December 2014 and January 2015 respectively. LT313 (LTZ 1313) is one of a pair that went on trial with Stagecoach Strathtay in the Dundee area in November 2014 before entering service in London. It was part of a batch of thirty-nine New Routemasters allocated to Stagecoach East London's Leyton garage to operate on route 55 between Oxford Circus and Bakers Arms, Leyton. LT313 is seen passing through Holborn, heading towards its final destination at Oxford Circus. (Liam Farrer-Beddall)

Brixton garage received a batch of forty New Routemasters over the winter of 2014 for route 137 (Streatham Hill–Oxford Circus). LT329 (LTZ 1329) represents this batch and is seen approaching a busy Hyde Park Corner. (Liam Farrer-Beddall)

Brixton garage initially had two batches allocated to it for operation on the 137 and 59. As with many other operators, the batches were intermixed between the different services operated from a particular garage. LT335 (LTZ 1335) is one of the first batch of vehicles allocated to the 137. It is seen about to work on route 59 (Streatham Hill, St Leonard's Avenue–King's Cross). It is the former location where this vehicle is seen, advertising Cadbury's Crunchie chocolate bar. (Liam Farrer-Beddall)

Marble Arch provides the backdrop to this photograph of LT336 (LTZ 1336). It is seen correctly operating route 137 just before heading down a busy Oxford Street, which is on the left-hand side of this photograph. (Liam Farrer-Beddall)

Both the 59 and 137 terminate at Brixton bus garage, which is shown as Streatham Hill, Telford Avenue, on the blinds. LT339 (LTZ 1339) is seen at this location advertising Tanqueray in a green and white livery. (Liam Farrer-Beddall)

Arriva London won the contract for route 48 (Walthamstow–London Bridge) and a handful of New Routemasters initially operated the service alongside Wright Eclipse Gemini 2-bodied machines. One of the vehicles transferred across was LT344 (LTZ 1344), which is seen exiting Walthamstow bus station while heading to London Bridge. (Liam Farrer-Beddall)

One of the brighter advertising liveries was applied to LT347 (LTZ 1347) in early November 2016. This was a short-lived campaign to promote the opening of the new Lego store in Leicester Square. This vehicle is seen rounding Marble Arch. (Liam Farrer-Beddall)

Originally part of the 137 order, LT353 (LTZ 1353) was transferred to Stamford Hill garage to assist with the conversion of route 73 (Stoke Newington–Victoria). It is seen on this service passing the back end of Buckingham Palace, near to journey's end at Victoria station. (Liam Farrer-Beddall)

LT356 was transferred for a third time to Ash Grove garage in June 2017 for use on route 48. This was the result of the curtailing of route 73 to Oxford Circus, reducing the PVR of the route. It is seen exiting Walthamstow bus station. (Liam Farrer-Beddall)

Route 55 (Bakers Arms, Leyton–Oxford Circus) was converted to New Routemaster operation in February 2015. LT357 (LTZ 1357) is the first of the larger batch of vehicles allocated to Stagecoach London for this service. The introduction of the white logos can be seen on this vehicle, which is found travelling along Oxford Street before reaching its terminus near Oxford Circus. (Liam Farrer-Beddall)

Oxford Street also finds LT363 (LTZ 1363), which is seen loading passengers for the short journey to Oxford Circus. The curve of the window for the centre staircase is clearly seen in this view. (Liam Farrer-Beddall)

LT366 (LTZ 1366) is seen passing Hackney Downs station while heading towards Oxford Circus station. The service will shortly pass through Hackney Central before meandering its way through the suburbs to the Central area. (Liam Farrer-Beddall)

Hackney also finds LT368 (LTZ 1368), this time heading towards Leyton, Bakers Arms. It is seen approaching Hackney Central station on Mare Street. (Liam Farrer-Beddall)

A wet Holborn finds LT372 (LTZ 1372) travelling towards Oxford Circus. This section of Holborn is busy with New Routemasters, working on routes 8, 38 and 55. LT372 is being pursued by another route 55 New Routemaster. (Liam Farrer-Beddall)

In this photograph we see another view of a New Routemaster bound for Oxford Circus travelling through Holborn. This time, LT377 (LTZ 1377) is seen promoting Sky Q in a predominantly white livery. (Liam Farrer-Beddall)

Stagecoach took stock of a second batch of NBfL machines in February 2015 for the conversion of route 55 (Oxford Circus– Bakers Arms, Leyton). LT389 (LTZ 1389) is seen passing under the London Overground lines at Hackney Central while heading towards Leyton. (Liam Farrer-Beddall)

Go-Ahead London's Blue Triangle division was successful in gaining the tender for route 15 (Trafalgar Square–Blackwall) from Stagecoach London in August 2017. Route 15 had been operated for a long period by Stagecoach London. The change of operator led to the transfer of the dedicated batch of New Routemasters to the Go-Ahead London fleet. LT394 (LTZ 1394) is seen heading towards Blackwall at the Aldwych, displaying the logos of its new operator. (Liam Farrer-Beddall)

Seen with its original operator, Stagecoach London, LT402 (LTZ 1402) is seen passing through Ludgate Circus while heading towards Trafalgar Square. Ludgate Circus is another busy area for New Routemasters, with routes 11, 15 and 76 passing through. (Liam Farrer-Beddall)

Displaying the more traditional 'Not in Service', LT404 (LTZ 1404) is seen rounding Trafalgar Square before heading to its stand on The Strand. The curves of the bodywork are clearly shown in this photograph. (Liam Farrer-Beddall)

Route 15 snakes its way from Blackwall Docklands Light Railway station through the City of London to its final destination at Trafalgar Square. LT409 (LTZ 1409) is seen travelling down Fleet Street as it heads towards the latter destination. The infamous 'Gherkin' can be seen in the background. (Liam Farrer-Beddall)

Route 12 (Dulwich Library–Oxford Circus) was converted to New Routemaster operation in March 2015. This route soaks up a PVR of thirty-six machines. This service is one of many that serve Trafalgar Square, the location of this photograph showing LT419 (LTZ 1419). (Liam Farrer-Beddall)

There are numerous New Routemaster services that can be found passing through many of London's suburbs. One such place is Peckham, where we find LT421 (LTZ 1421) approaching the town centre. (Liam Farrer-Beddall)

As well as numerous products, London buses have also been used on many occasions to promote a number of films and West End stage shows. One such example is LT424 (LTZ 1424), which is seen promoting the James Bond film *Spectre*. This vehicle wore this advertising wrap for a couple of months in the autumn of 2015. (Liam Farrer-Beddall)

LT429 (LTZ 1429) is seen travelling through Haymarket having not long left the Oxford Circus terminus. Other examples of Wright products can be seen following this example. (Liam Farrer-Beddall)

One of the brighter advertising liveries applied to the New Routemaster was found on LT436 (LTZ 1436). This vehicle was used to advertise yet another film, this time the animated *Trolls* movie. Carrying this livery between September and December 2016, this vehicle is seen passing through Elephant and Castle. (Liam Farrer-Beddall)

A busy Trafalgar Square finds LT443 (LTZ 1443) travelling towards Dulwich Library. It is closely followed fellow Go-Ahead London LT293 (LTZ 1293) operating a 453 service to Deptford Bridge. The two services follow each other as far as Elephant and Castle before going their separate ways. (Liam Farrer-Beddall)

Peckham town centre finds LT447 (LTZ 1447) heading for Oxford Circus. Route 12 travels from Dulwich Library to Oxford Circus via Peckham, Camberwell and Elephant and Castle. (Liam Farrer-Beddall)

A handful of NBfL routes pass over Westminster Bridge, with route 12 being one of them. The Houses of Parliament provide the backdrop to this photograph of LT451 (LTZ 1451) as it heads towards Dulwich Library in South East London from Oxford Circus. (Liam Farrer-Beddall)

A second advertising campaign for Wall's Magnum lolly was applied to a number of New Routemasters in 2016. This time, leopard print on a black background was used. This can be seen clearly on LT456 (LTZ 1456), which is captured travelling through Trafalgar Square towards Marylebone on route 453. (Liam Farrer-Beddall)

Trafalgar Square finds LT458 (LTZ 1458) travelling towards Camden Town on route 88. The batch intended for the 88 is often intermixed with those operated on route 11. Both services are operated from Go-Ahead London's Stockwell garage. (Liam Farrer-Beddall)

LT461 (LTZ 1461) was one of two, the other being LT460, built to help cover an increase in the PVR on routes 148 and 9 with London United. LT460 found itself allocated to Shepherds Bush garage, while LT461 was added to Stamford Brook's allocation. Trafalgar Square is the location of this photograph. (Liam Farrer-Beddall)

March 2015 saw another pair of New Routemasters delivered to London, this time to Stagecoach London for route 15. They followed on from the additional examples delivered to London United, being numbered LT462/3. LT462 (LTZ 1462) is seen rounding Trafalgar Square while heading out on route 15 to Blackwall. (Liam Farrer-Beddall)

LT465 (LTZ 1465) formed part of the original batch of New Routemasters that were allocated to route 73. A service reduction on the 73 led to the reallocation of some of the vehicles from this service to route 48 (Walthamstow Central–London Bridge). LT465 is seen about to enter Walthamstow Central bus station. (Liam Farrer-Beddall)

Route 254 (Nags Head, Holloway–Aldgate) was another service to benefit from New Routemasters being displaced from service reductions on other services. LT474 (LTZ 1474) is seen travelling near to Hackney Downs Overground station, bound for Holloway. (Liam Farrer-Beddall)

Walthamstow bus station is seen in the background of this photograph of LT475 (LTZ 1475), which is seen traveling through on rail replacement duties, terminating just up the road from where it is seen. The New Routemasters are commonly used on rail replacement services at weekends when service levels are reduced. LT475 was another example that formed the first half of the route 73 allocation. (Liam Farrer-Beddall)

Route 88 was converted to New Routemaster operation in August 2015. Seen soon after delivery, LT484 (LTZ 1484) passes through Trafalgar Square. The batch are allocated to Stockwell garage and can commonly be found operating on route 11. (Liam Farrer-Beddall)

The familiar background of King's Cross station is seen here. A number of New Routemaster services pass by King's Cross to various parts of London. LT494 (LTZ 1494) is seen here heading towards Victoria on route 73. This service was later cut back to Oxford Circus. (Liam Farrer-Beddall)

Stamford Hill-based LT495 (LTZ 1495) is seen entering Euston bus station from Euston Road. The SF garage code can be seen just behind the front wheel. Seen bound for its final destination at Stoke Newington, this bus formed part of the second batch of New Routemasters allocated to route 73. (Liam Farrer-Beddall)

The middle numbered New Routemaster is LT500. This vehicle is seen travelling down Oxford Street towards Victoria. (Liam Farrer-Beddall)

Whitehall is another busy thoroughfare for the New Routemaster, as can be seen in this photograph. The tower of Big Ben can be seen in the background of this shot of LT506 (LTZ 1506), which is operating route 11 instead of the intended route 88. (Gary Seamarks).

Like route 73, the New Routemasters allocated to route 88 were also delivered in two different batches. Representing the second batch is LT507 (LTZ 1507), which is seen passing through Trafalgar Square. (Liam Farrer-Beddall)

As previously mentioned, the New Routemasters allocated to route 88 are allocated to Stockwell garage, and therefore can be used on route 11. Illustrating this point is LT511 (LTZ 1511), which is seen passing through Victoria towards Fulham Broadway. (Liam Farrer-Beddall)

The East London location of East Ham is an area that has no official New Routemaster services passing through it. However, this is the location of LT514 (LTZ 1514), which is seen operating a rail replacement service to Walthamstow Central, showing the appropriate blinds. (Liam Farrer-Beddall)

Arriva London's route 149 (Edmonton Green–London Bridge) was converted from DW-class Wrightbus integral machines to the New Routemasters in October 2015. LT516 (LTZ 1516) was delivered to Arriva London in November 2015 and was put to use on the 149. It is seen having just loaded at Bishopsgate in the City of London, before completing its journey to London Bridge. (Liam Farrer-Beddall)

Having just left the stop for King's Cross station, LT517 (LTZ 1517) is seen displaying the new destination for route 73 (Oxford Circus). It is about to pass the infamous Central London rail terminal before passing St Pancras and Euston rail stations on its way to journey's end. (Liam Farrer-Beddall)

The double rail bridge carrying the main line into King's Cross at Finsbury Park provides the backdrop for this photograph of LT522 (LTZ 1522). It is seen heading towards Hackney Central on route 253. LT522 was one of a split batch of vehicles allocated to route 73 at Stamford Hill, but can be found on either the 73 or 253. (Liam Farrer-Beddall)

The inter-working of routes 73 and 253 is illustrated in this image of LT529 (LTZ 1529). As can be gathered by the application of the 'SF' garage code just before the front staircase, the routes are operated from Stamford Hill garage. Euston bus station is the southern terminus of route 253, which travels to Hackney Central. The National Rail and London Underground logos attached to the terminal building at Euston can be seen just in front of the vehicle. (Liam Farrer-Beddall)

Another Central location that numerous New Routemaster services pass through is Park Lane. LT533 (LTZ 1533) is seen negotiating a busy Park Lane while operating route 73 to Stoke Newington. (Liam Farrer-Beddall)

Another white-based all-over advertising livery was applied to the New Routemaster to promote Vans shoes. LT534 (LTZ 1534) is seen carrying this livery in March 2016 while passing through Marble Arch, bound for Victoria on the 73. (Gary Seamarks)

Park Lane also finds LT538 (LTZ 1538). This vehicle was decorated in the green bus livery soon after delivery to London. This was the first generation of London buses to gain such adverts to promote the numerous London buses that were fitted with green technology. (Liam Farrer-Beddall)

Metroline allocated their New Routemaster machines to either Cricklewood or Holloway garages. Cricklewood operated services 16, 168 and 189, and route 16 was the first of these three to be taken over by the new type. The arrival of three batches saw a common user pool of vehicles to operate the trio of services. One such example is LT544 (LTZ 1544). Originally taken into stock for route 16, it is seen passing through Waterloo on route 168. (Liam Farrer-Beddall)

Metroline's LT553 (LTZ 1553) is seen at the stop for Marble Arch station on Edgware Road, just before negotiating Marble Arch and heading towards Victoria via Park Lane. This photograph can now be classed as an archive shot as the Odeon cinema in the background is no longer there. (Liam Farrer-Beddall)

Seen on the correct service is LT558 (LTZ 1558), which is travelling down Park Lane before entering Marble Arch on route 16. This route is one of a number of Metroline services that terminate at the company's Cricklewood garage. The background of this photograph shows the Park Lane Hotel at the Hyde Park Corner end of the road. (Liam Farrer-Beddall)

Displaying the incorrect terminating point, LT559 (LTZ 1559) is displaying the old destination of Oxford Circus for route 189. Marble Arch is the location of this photograph, as the 189 runs between Marble Arch and Brent Cross Shopping Centre. The difference in the Metroline logo can be seen in this photograph when compared with an earlier Metroline LT in this book. (Liam Farrer-Beddall)

Another shot showing off the three-doored layout of the New Routemaster. LT560 (LTZ 1560) is seen rounding Marble Arch bound for Cricklewood garage. It will soon travel up Edgeware Road and cross Marylebone Road before travelling through Kilburn. (Liam Farrer-Beddall)

For the majority of its journey, route 149 travels almost in a straight line from Shoreditch to Edmonton Green. LT564 (LTZ 1564) is seen passing through Dalston as it heads towards the northern terminus at Edmonton Green. (Liam Farrer-Beddall)

Seen about to enter Edmonton Green bus station is LT582 (LTZ 1582), which is about to start its day's work on route 149 to London Bridge. (Liam Farrer-Beddall)

LT602 (LTZ 1602) was the first of thirty-nine examples taken into stock by Abellio London in November 2015 for the conversion of route 159 (Streatham Hill–Marble Arch). The 159 was the last service to see operation of the traditional AEC Routemaster bus, with the last of these vehicles operating the service in December 2005. Bays adjacent to Hyde Park provides layover bays for the numerous New Routemaster routes that terminate at Marble Arch, which is the location of this photograph. (Liam Farrer-Beddall)

LT609 (LTZ 1609) is seen pulling off the stop at Bond Street Underground station on Oxford Street, shortly before arriving at Marble Arch. The entrance seen underneath the blue Underground sign leads into a shopping centre, as well as the Tube station. (Liam Farrer-Beddall)

The other end of route 159 is illustrated here. A parking ground adjacent to Streatham station provides enough space for a number of New Routemasters on the 159, as well as some other London routes. LT619 (LTZ 1619) is seen loading before starting its journey into Central London. (Liam Farrer-Beddall)

The Abellio New Routemasters found themselves allocated to Battersea garage. As is typical with the type, they again formed a common user pool. When routes 211 (Waterloo–Hammersmith) and 3 (Crystal Palace–Oxford Circus) were converted to the type, the 159 batch found themselves frequently operating these other services. Demonstrating this is LT623 (LTZ 1623), which is seen passing the Greenline terminal in Victoria while operating a 211 service to Hammersmith. (Liam Farrer-Beddall)

Another shot of a New Routemaster taken at Streatham Station terminus. This time, LT634 (LTZ 1634) is seen awaiting its next journey to Marble Arch. However, the destination display has not been updated for this inbound journey. (Liam Farrer-Beddall)

Another of the route 159 New Routemasters is captured off route. This time LT640 (LTZ 1640) is seen passing through Trafalgar Square on Abellio's other NRM service at the time, route 3. This particular journey has been cut short from Oxford Circus to Piccadilly Circus. (Liam Farrer-Beddall)

A further twenty-three NRMs were taken into stock by Metroline in December 2015 to operate service 168 (Hampstead Heath–Old Kent Road). Based at Cricklewood, these vehicles can be found on any of the New Routemaster services from that garage. LT643 is seen heading through Kilburn High Road while operating route 16 to Victoria in an all-over advertising wrap for Sky Q. (Liam Farrer-Beddall)

Seen on the intended route is LT650 (LTZ 1650), which is photographed crossing Waterloo Bridge on a 168 journey to Hampstead Heath. The service was won from Arriva London, replacing Wright Eclipse Gemini-bodied Volvo B7TL machines from this service. (Liam Farrer-Beddall)

Seen travelling in the opposite direction is LT652 (LTZ 1652). Waterloo is again the location of this photograph, but this time it is seen near the IMAX Cinema, a reflection of which can be seen on the upper deck of this vehicle. (Liam Farrer-Beddall)

In this view we see LT655 (LTZ 1655) a bit further along the route at Elephant and Castle. It is seen sporting a blank destination display and the 'W' garage code worn by many Cricklewood-based vehicles. (Liam Farrer-Beddall)

Seen just starting a service on route 16 is LT659 (LTZ 1659), which is busy negotiating various building works in the Victoria area of Central London. Another New Routemaster can just be glimpsed in the very back of the photograph, along with a Plaxton President and an Enviro 400 machine. (Liam Farrer-Beddall)

A Christmassy Euston bus station finds LT665 (LTZ 1665) on a dark winter's evening. This vehicle was one of twenty-seven examples to have been taken into stock by Go-Ahead London for operation on route 68 (Euston–West Norwood), with that route allocated to Camberwell garage. This photograph is filled with Wrightbus products, with two Gemini models visible. (Liam Farrer-Beddall)

For a couple of months over the winter of 2017, Go-Ahead London's LT669 (LTZ 1669) carried a stylish all-over advertisement for Delta Airlines on a light blue background. The windows on the lower deck were given vinyls to look like the windows of an aircraft. It is seen passing through Tennison Way, Waterloo, bound for Euston station. (Liam Farrer-Beddall)

Seen negotiating Waterloo while heading northbound towards Euston on a 68 service is LT676 (LTZ 1676). A comparison between the New Routemaster and the ADL Enviro 400 can be made in this view. (Liam Farrer-Beddall)

Waterloo Bridge provides a good location for photographing the London skyline. Among the buildings competing for attention in this view of LT678 (LTZ 1678) are The Shard and the London Studios. (Gary Seamarks)

The Waterloo IMAX Cinema can be seen much more clearly in this image of LT683 (LTZ 1683). To the right of the photograph, the former Royal Waterloo Hospital for Women and Children can also be seen. LT683 is captured heading towards its southern terminus at West Norwood. (Liam Farrer-Beddall)

Route 68 was the second New Routemaster route to transfer across to another operator. Go-Ahead London lost the service to Abellio London, with the fleet of NRMs crossing the road from Camberwell garage to Walworth. Displaying the change of ownership is LT688 (LTZ 1688), which is seen sporting its new owner's fleet names while being held at a traffic light at Elephant and Castle. (Liam Farrer-Beddall)

Putney is another area of London that is not served by any New Routemaster routes. However, Abellio London's LT699 (LTZ 1699) is seen about to cross Putney Bridge on a rail replacement service for the London Underground. (Liam Farrer-Beddall)

Another all-over advertising NRM was LT704 (LTZ 1704), which is seen carrying a blue-based livery for Tommy Hilfiger. This was one of twenty-five NRMs taken into stock to operate route 3 between Piccadilly Circus and Crystal Palace. (Liam Farrer-Beddall)

Hammersmith bus station finds LT709 (LTZ 1709) in an all-over advertising livery for Replay Jeans Store in Carnaby Street, a livery worn over the winter of 2017. It is seen in between duties, waiting to operate a 211 service back to Waterloo station. (Liam Farrer-Beddall)

Trafalgar Square finds LT713 (LTZ 1713) heading towards Crystal Palace. A comparison between the New Routemaster and fellow Wright-manufactured Eclipse Gemini 2 model can be made in this photograph. (Liam Farrer-Beddall)

Nike ran an advertising campaign on several New Routemasters between October 2017 and January 2018. One such vehicle was LT717 (LTZ 1717), which is seen about to pick up at Waterloo. (Liam Farrer-Beddall)

Arriva London took delivery of twenty-nine New Routemasters in March and April 2016 for route 59 (Streatham Hill–King's Cross). Allocated to Brixton garage, the vehicles were also found on route 137, with the 137 batch being found on the 59. LT718 (LTZ 1718) is seen passing through Marble Arch on an Oxford Circus-bound 137. (Liam Farrer-Beddall)

LT723 (LTZ 1723) is seen at journey's end at Telford Avenue, Streatham Hill (Brixton bus garage), having just completed a 59 service from King's Cross. The service uses Brixton garage to turn around before setting off on another journey to Central London. (Liam Farrer-Beddall)

On its way to King's Cross, route 59 passes through Waterloo, the location of this photograph. LT724 (LTZ 1724) is seen about to make a stop at the Tennison Way set of bus stops. The rail line in the background runs to Charing Cross rail terminal, serving the smaller Waterloo East station rather than the main Waterloo station. (Liam Farrer-Beddall)

The artificial orange lights of Euston bus station can be seen reflecting on the roof of LT735 (LTZ 1735), which is departing Euston and heading for Telford Avenue, Streatham Hill. (Liam Farrer-Beddall)

Holloways route 91 (Crouch End–Trafalgar Square) is one route that has a tendency to keep the designated batch of New Routemasters operating it, with a few straying onto routes 24 and 390. The stand for the 91 is on Northumberland Avenue, just off Trafalgar Square. This is the location of LT749 (LTZ 1749), which is seen blinded for the 91 to Crouch End. (Liam Farrer-Beddall)

After leaving its stand, route 91 has to negotiate the majority of the Trafalgar Square roundabout to reach The Strand. LT755 (LTZ 1755) is seen almost halfway round promoting YouTube, another white-based all-over advertising livery applied to New Routemasters. (Liam Farrer-Beddall)

Route 211 (Waterloo–Hammersmith) was converted to the type in June 2016. Seen on its intended service is LT772 (LTZ 1772). It is passing Victoria coach station on Buckingham Palace Road while heading towards Hammersmith. (Liam Farrer-Beddall)

A sunny Marble Arch finds LT776 (LTZ 1776) on layover before starting another journey back to Streatham station. This photograph again demonstrates the fluidity of the batches of New Routemasters operating with Abellio London from Battersea garage. (Liam Farrer-Beddall)

Victoria coach station provides the background of this photograph, with LT779 (LTZ 1779) heading towards Waterloo station on route 211. The 211 terminates on Station Approach, sharing a stand with route 507. (Liam Farrer-Beddall)

Seen on Station Approach at Waterloo is LT787 (LTZ 1787). It is parked up on layover before setting out on another journey to Hammersmith bus station. (Liam Farrer-Beddall)

Cricklewood garage took stock of twenty-three New Routemasters to operate route 189. LT797 (LTZ 1797) is seen loading at Victoria bus station while having a day out on the 16. (Liam Farrer-Beddall)

Originally numbered ST2001 (LTZ 2001), ST812 (LTZ 1812) was the smallest of the New Routemasters to have been built. It is almost a metre shorter than the standard LT class. It was originally built to this specification to combat some issues encountered with the turning circle at Crouch End Broadway. However, this was the only one of this length made, the other 999 New Routemasters being of a standard length. Metroline's Holloway garage is where this vehicle was allocated. It is seen parked on Northumberland Avenue. (Liam Farrer-Beddall)

LT813 (LTZ 1813) was one of thirty-three New Routemasters taken into stock by Arriva London at Stamford Hill to work route 253 (Euston–Hackney Central). However, this vehicle is seen operating a journey on route 73, passing King's Cross as it heads towards Stoke Newington. (Liam Farrer-Beddall)

King's Cross also finds LT815 (LTZ 1815) operating route 73 towards Stoke Newington. It is seen having just loaded at the stops seen in the background. The frontage of King's Cross station is on the right side of this photograph, while St Pancras provides the left-hand view. (Liam Farrer-Beddall)

A third example of the '253' batch is seen exiting a wet Euston bus station – LT819 (LTZ 1819). Again, this vehicle is operating route 73. (Liam Farrer-Beddall)

Euston bus station also finds LT832 (LTZ 1832), this time operating a 253 service to Hackney Central. Euston is as far into Central London as the 253 travels, passing through areas such as Finsbury Park and Manor House before reaching its destination at Hackney Central. (Liam Farrer-Beddall)

No less than 109 consecutive New Routemasters were delivered to Go-Ahead London's London Central, London General and Blue Triangle operations between October 2016 and March 2017. They took up service on five routes, the 21, 76 and EL1–3. LT845 (LTZ 1845) was the first example to arrive in October. It is seen loading at London Bridge while operating a shortened journey on the 21 to Moorgate. (Liam Farrer-Beddall)

Route 21 passes through part of the City of London, which provides the backdrop for this photograph. The infamous 'Cheesegrater' and 'Walkie Talkie' skyscrapers are prominent above LT850 (LTZ 1850) as it crosses London Bridge, having just exited the 'Square Mile' soon after delivery. (Liam Farrer-Beddall)

Route 21 runs between Lewisham Shopping Centre and Newington Green. Seen passing under the rail bridge near Lewisham station is LT860 (LTZ 1860). The three-door layout of the NBfL can be clearly discerned in the photograph. (Liam Farrer-Beddall)

Seen rounding a corner near the former Lewisham bus station is LT864 (LTZ 1864), which is nearing journey's end at Lewisham Shopping Centre. (Liam Farrer-Beddall)

Route 76 (Waterloo–Tottenham Hale bus station) was converted to NRM operation in March 2017. The route travels through a number of busy locations, including Dalston Junction. This is where we find LT879 (LTZ 1879), one of the intended batch for the 76. The NRMs for the 76, EL1, EL2 and EL3 were initially mixed up, being split between the four routes. (Liam Farrer-Beddall)

Seen at the southern end of route 76, at Waterloo, is LT890 (LTZ 1890). The route requires twenty-five vehicles at peak times. (Liam Farrer-Beddall)

A mix up with the allocation of the East London Transit batch and those introduced on route 76 saw examples from the two batches being mixed between the four services. LT892 (LTZ 1892) was one vehicle for the 76 but is seen at Barking station, operating an EL3 service towards Little Heath. (Liam Farrer-Beddall)

Ninety-nine of the final 100 NRMs are registered in a slightly different registration sequence: LTZ 2101–99. Representing the first of the batch is LT901 (LTZ 2101), one of many used on the East London Transit network centred on Barking. It is seen passing Barking station on an EL1 service towards Ilford station. (Liam Farrer-Beddall)

EL1 runs between Ilford station and Barking Riverside. LT904 (LTZ 2104) is seen passing through Ilford, having just started its journey out to Barking. EL1 is the only New Routemaster service to operate into Ilford. (Liam Farrer-Beddall)

Showing the mix up in route 76 and East London Transit batches of NRMs is LT908 (LTZ 2108). This vehicle was intended for the Blue Triangle operation on the EL1–3 group of services. It is, however, seen operating London General's route 76, passing through Dalston. (Liam Farrer-Beddall)

The East London Transit services centred on the Barking area saw a large batch of fifty NRM machines enter service from the River Road, Barking garage, with Blue Triangle. Initially, the batch stayed in East London, but after the transfer of route 15 from Stagecoach to Blue Triangle the batch became a regular sight in Central London. LT914 (LTZ 2114) is seen nearing journey's end as it passed through Aldwych. The dedicated East London Transit livery can clearly be seen on this vehicle. (Liam Farrer-Beddall).

Another view of the special East London Transit livery, which is being worn by LT916 (LTZ 2116). The bus is seen approaching the Barking station stop on its journey from Ilford station to Barking Riverside. (Liam Farrer-Beddall)

Barking station provides the backdrop to LT936 (LTZ 2136), which is operating service EL2 to Beacontree Heath, and the East London Transit livery can be clearly seen in this photograph. The fleet number on this batch of vehicles is situated below the drivers' window rather than above it. (Liam Farrer-Beddall)

Route 137 was cut back from Oxford Circus to Marble Arch to help reduce the amount of buses travelling down Oxford Street. To help slightly improve air quality in Central London, the original LT3** batch of NRMs were replaced by thirty newer examples. This was the penultimate batch of New Routemasters delivered to London. LT957 (LTZ 2157) is seen travelling through Hyde Park Corner, destined for Marble Arch. (Liam Farrer-Beddall)

Numerous NRM routes serve Marble Arch. The curtailment of route 137 saw the 159 NRMs share the stands with the 137, and later the 189. Pictured finding a place to park is LT958 (LTZ 2158), which is wearing an all-over advertisement for American Express. (Liam Farrer-Beddall)

The winter of 2017/18 saw a temporary theatre built at Marble Arch. This can be seen in the left-hand side of this photograph of LT965 (LTZ 2165), which is about to embark on another journey to Brixton bus garage, also known as Telford Avenue, Streatham Hill. (Liam Farrer-Beddall)

The route 137 batch frequently see service on route 59. Demonstrating this is LT979 (LTZ 2179), which has just started a journey to Streatham Hill at King's Cross. (Liam Farrer-Beddall)

The last batch of NRMs were allocated to London United's Fulwell garage in West London. They were placed into service on route 267 between Fulwell and Hammersmith in November 2017. LT984 (LTZ 2184) is the first example numerically of the batch; it is seen passing through Twickenham as it heads towards Fulwell. (Liam Farrer-Beddall)

Seen starting a journey to Fulwell is LT995 (LTZ 2195). Photographed exiting a wet Hammersmith bus station, it will then head past the Hammersmith Apollo. (Liam Farrer-Beddall)

Since their introduction, the New Routemaster have attended the annual spring gathering of the London Bus Museum at Brooklands. The final example, LT1000 (LTZ 1000), is seen operating the special 462 service between the Brooklands Museum site and Weybridge station. It is at the latter location when captured. (Liam Farrer-Beddall)

It is necessary to illustrate the unique rear end styling of the New Routemaster. The front shots provided throughout the book show how curvy the type is at the front and sides. This pattern continues at the rear of the vehicle, with a curvy rear roof area. The second staircase at the rear of the vehicle can also be seen in this image. The line of the staircase is mirrored by the window, giving the passenger a view as they use it. LT184 and LT367 are the subjects of this photograph, which was taken in Hackney Central. (Liam Farrer-Beddall)

The grand St Pancras Hotel is the main focus of this photograph, the building itself overshadowing LT473 (LTZ 1473). The New Routemaster is seen operating a 73 service to Stoke Newington on a summer Saturday morning. (Liam Farrer-Beddall)

The Wright SRM model differs from the NBfL by having only one staircase and the standard two doors common to London buses. At the front, the vehicle looks identical to the NBfL, but the rear is very different, being flat and more box-like, as well as missing a third door. London Sovereign took stock of six examples in 2016, initially for use on route 13 into Central London. After the loss of the service, the vehicles were redeployed on the 183 between Golders Green and Pinner. VHR 45207 (LJ66 EZT) is seen exiting Harrow bus station en route to Golders Green. (Liam Farrer-Beddall)

The future? One of a pair of Wright SRM-bodied Volvo B5LHC machies was exhibited at the Buses Festival 2017. A white pod can be seen on the roof of this vehicle, and this is to be the site of a pantograph for charging the vehicle. The pair have now been allocated to Go-Ahead London at Peckham garage, and numbered VHP1 and VHP2 respectively. (Luke Garley)